gymnastics

the
SUMMER OLYMPICS

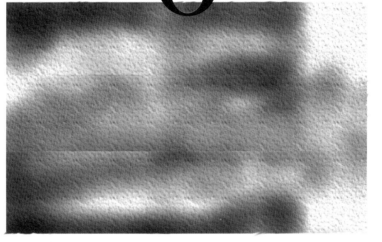

gymnastics

PUBLISHED BY SMART APPLE MEDIA

Published by Smart Apple Media
123 South Broad Street, Mankato, Minnesota 56001

Cover Illustration by Eric Melhorn

Designed by Core Design

Photos by: Bettmann Archives, Sports Photo Masters
and Wide World Photos

Library of Congress Cataloging-in-Publication Data

Smale, David.
Gymnastics / by David Smale.
(The Summer Olympics)
Includes index.
Summary: Provides an overview of gymnastics
competition at the Olympics.

ISBN 1-887068-00-7

1. Gymnastics—Juvenile literature. 2. Olympics—
Juvenile literature. [1. Gymnastics—History. 2.
Olympics.] I. Title. II. Series.

GV461.S58 1995   95-11965
796.44—dc20

AN OLYMPIC FAVORITE

Running, flipping and twisting, gymnasts whirl across the screens of the world's televisions every four years during Olympic competition. From the tiny ballerina-like dancers in the women's floor exercise to the strong, sturdy men on the rings, gymnasts are among the most watched and admired of all Olympic athletes.

Women's gymnastics is one of the most popular Olympic sports.

Vitaly Scherbo won six gold medals in 1992.

In a 1984 poll, Americans were asked which Olympic sport they would watch if they could choose only one. Women's gymnastics was chosen by a majority of those polled.

With the 1996 Olympics in Atlanta quickly approaching, the world waits to see the next stars of women's and men's gymnastics. Perhaps there will be another Olga Korbut, Nadia Comaneci or Mary Lou Retton to dazzle the crowd. And in the men's competition, a new group of thick-armed challengers will be vying for Olympic gold.

WORLD-CLASS ACROBATS

Men's Olympic gymnastics competition began in the 1896 Athens Games in Paris. Over the years, the number of events in men's gymnastics has changed. Some of the events that have been contested at various times that are no longer included are the rope climb, club swinging, side horse vault and tumbling.

Since 1936 men have competed in six events: long horse vault, high bar, parallel bars, pommel horse, rings and floor exercise. All of the gymnasts compete in compulsory and optional exercises for the team competition. The total scores of the top five gymnasts for each country are added to determine a country's total score. The top six gymnasts in each event go on to compete in the individual events and in the all-around competition, which

The men's long horse vault (pages 10-11).

determines the best athletes in the six events combined. In 1984 the rules were changed so that no more than two athletes from one country could compete in the all-around and individual events.

Prior to 1952, women gymnasts competed only in team combined exercises in three Olympics: Amsterdam in 1928, Berlin in 1936 and London in 1948. At the 1952 Olympics in Helsinki, women started competing in four events—uneven parallel bars,

Women perform compulsory floor exercises to music.

vault, balance beam and floor exercise—in team competition, all-around competition and individual apparatus. This format continues to be followed today.

MEN'S INDIVIDUAL EVENTS

The six events that make up the men's competition cover a wide variety of skills. Speed is a key ingredient in the long horse vault. The athlete races at top speed toward a padded beam approximately 53 inches (135 cm) off the ground. Right before he reaches it, he hits a springboard and pushes off the vault with his hands to produce a variety of flips and turns. It is critical that he lands with his feet together and his legs straight.

In the high bar, the gymnast swings from a horizontal bar 102 inches (259 cm) off the ground. He is required to per-

A gymnast performs a routine on the pommel horse.

form various maneuvers. Again, he must hit the ground with both feet together.

The parallel bars are slightly more than body-width apart and are 67 inches (170 cm) from the floor. The gymnast swings between, over and around the bars, sometimes coming to a complete stop in a V shape and at other times flipping all around. The gymnast needs very strong arms for this event, as all of his

Gymnastics requires strength and flexibility.

and claimed four more gold medals in the rings, pommel horse, vault and parallel bars, for a total of six gold medals.

The Soviet and Japanese men have dominated the team competition in the Olympics since 1952. Between 1952 and 1976, these two countries finished first or second in every team competition. In the all-around competition, no other country won a medal except in 1984, when the Soviet Union boycotted the Games.

Alberto Braglia captured the gold in 1908 and 1912.

The Americans seized their opportunity in 1984, claiming the gold medal on their home turf in Los Angeles. In fact, three of the six men (Peter Vidmar, Mitch Gaylord and Timothy Daggett) had competed in Pauley Pavilion, the site of the competition, during their collegiate careers. The Americans edged the Chinese in a close competition, while the Japanese settled for the bronze.

WOMEN'S INDIVIDUAL EVENTS

The four events that make up the women's competition are not that different from the men's events. The women also have a vault, but the horse is turned sideways. Since most of the competitors are quite small, the vaulting horse is nearly as tall as the gymnasts themselves.

In the uneven parallel bars the top bar is about 90 inches (229 cm) high, while the lower bar is about 60 inches (152 cm) high; the bars are approximately 36 inches (91 cm) apart. The gymnast swings from one to the other, sometimes performing flips off of one and grabbing the other bar just before hitting the ground.

The floor exercise for women is similar to the men's, except that the women perform their tumbling routines to music. The balance beam is an event that is unique to the women. The beam is approximately 4 inches (10 cm) wide, 16 feet 4 inches (5 m)

long and about 4 feet (1.22 m) off the ground. Gymnasts walk, jump and flip back and forth on the beam, sometimes using their hands and other times their feet.

INSTANT STARDOM

With women's gymnastics being so popular, it's no wonder that it's the young women who are the stars.

Charismatic Olga Korbut put women's gymnastics in the spotlight.

Olga Korbut was a 17-year-old who looked half that age as the 1972 Olympics began. She stood only 4-foot-11 (1.5 m) and weighed just 85 pounds (38.6 kg). On the first day of competition in Munich, Korbut performed so well that many people were talking about her as a possible all-around champion, even though she had only made the powerful Soviet team as an alternate. But on the second day, she fell off the uneven parallel bars and scored a 7.5, which ended her chances of a medal.

The next day, when the competition began in the individual events, Korbut was back in form. She took the silver in the very event in which she had fallen the day before, then won both the balance beam and the floor exercise. With her spirit and her charismatic smile, Korbut changed women's gymnastics forever.

Judges award points for technical difficulty, form and continuity.

In the 1976 Olympics in Montreal, much of the world's attention was focused on the Soviets—Korbut, reigning world champion Lyudmila Tourischeva and rising star Nelli Kim. But Nadia Comaneci of Romania stole the show. During the team competition, the 4-foot-11 (1.5 m) Comaneci made history, scoring the first perfect 10s in Olympic competition, doing so on the uneven parallel bars and the balance beam. Before the Games were over, she recorded seven more perfect scores. She not only won the all-around competition, but she also won gold on the uneven bars and the balance beam.

The next star in women's gymnastics was American Mary Lou Retton. Retton was a compact 16-year-old from West Virginia who took advantage of the Soviet-led boycott of the 1984 Olympics in Los Angeles by grabbing the all-around gold and helping her team win the silver in team competition. No American woman had ever won an individual medal in Olympic gymnastics competition before Retton. In fact, none had ever finished in the top eight in the all-around competition and only one had been in the top six in any individual competition (Linda Metheny, 1968 balance beam).

After Retton, Americans were given a chance in Olympic competition. In 1992 in Barcelona, Kim Zmeskal of Houston was a favorite for the all-around before she fell off the balance beam; it seemed to affect her performance the rest of the competition. Step-

The pommel horse demands total concentration (pages 26-27).

ping in for the Americans was Shannon Miller, who won four individual medals (including a silver in the all-around competition) and a bronze team medal. She will be a favorite in Atlanta.

MORE COMPETITION TO FLIP OVER

When the United States hosts the 1996 Olympic Games in Atlanta, it will be the second time in 12 years that the Olympics will be on American soil. Will there be another Mary Lou Retton for the United States? Will there be a surprise winner in the team competition for the men or the women? What will the breakup of the Soviet Union mean in the team competition?

The age at which many gymnasts, especially the women,

The world's top athletes will be reaching for the gold in 1996.

reach their peak makes it difficult to predict who will be the next great champion. But one thing is certain: there will be plenty of gymnasts flying through the air, employing strength, grace and concentration to achieve their goals and delighting all who watch.

No matter who takes the gold, the fans always win.

gymnastics

Gold Medal Winners in 1992

Men

Event	Winner	Nation
All-around	Vitaly Scherbo	Unified Team
Long horse vault	Vitaly Scherbo	Unified Team
Pommel horse	(tie) Vitaly Scherbo and Pae Gil Su	Unified Team North Korea
Horizontal bar	Trent Dimas	United States
Parallel bars	Vitaly Scherbo	Unified Team
Rings	Vitaly Scherbo	Unified Team
Floor exercise	Li Xiaosahuang	China
Team	Unified Team	

Women

All-around	Tatiana Gutsu	Unified Team
Balance beam	Tatiana Lisenko	Unified Team
Uneven parallel bars	Lu Li	China
Side horse vault	(tie) Henrietta Onodi and Lavinia Milosovici	Hungary Romania
Floor exercise	Lavinia Milosovici	Romania
Team	Unified Team	
Rhythmic	Aleksandra Timoshenko	Unified Team

RECORDS

INDEX